Poems from a Land Girl

Neva MacDonald-Haig MBE

SUNSET

The air is still this evening
While the sun is going to bed
Lighting the hills with his colour,
Dying the clouds with his head;
And as he slips lower and lower
And as he sinks into the sea,
His beams form a glittering pathway
That stretches from him right to me.
And I think how you travelled that pathway
That leads from the night to the day,
And you left me alone in the darkness,
In a world that was weary and gray.
Yet I see you again in the evening,
When I see that path of light –
But you leave me once more in the darkness
When the sun sinks out of sight.

1939

3

AN AUTUMN NIGHT

...But still I ride
                    And still I long for you
The air is cold with rain; the road
Shines in the yellow moonlight. Soft grey mist
Hushes the swish of tyres and the hollow beat of
The horses hooves. Voices sound still and far,
 Or rustle quickly – living in the grayness.
The life of noise is conquered by the mist of night
Subdued and silenced by the moisture – beading
Shifting, clinging curtain of opaqueness -
Dream filled I ride, charged with thoughts that find their waking
When the frank sky is hidden and the air is brooding
deepening – changed – a lonely dog
Barks sharply, shattering the dark grey calm
Of fields and rain, and rather frightened darkness.
...But still I ride
                    And still I long for you...

1943

This poem was written when Sandy my husband was overseas at war in Burma.
We were married for 10 days and he was away for 3 years.

Sandy Home – Aberlour!

TO PETER – MY BROTHER

A Pilot thunders through the desolate skies,
Only a sound, but memory takes us there.
We were not with you on your last long flight,
At least, of course you know, our hearts were there.

And then we see you grave, until your eyes
Light up – you know we loved your smile! 'Twas right
That God should give you that, to let us share.

You laugh at that, but then of course you would
You were so gay, and yet so kind and fair.
And while you lived and smiled, and waked and slept
This family was complete, 'cos you were there.

And when we talked and read, or rode, or swam, you
could Love and laugh with us – and if we wept
You couldn't understand, but you were there.

Gladly you lived indeed, Life was your friend. The foam
Of evening was not spread against the tide
Of heav'n when He hushed your engine's drone.

And as you loved through space to soar and fly
On eagles wings He bore you through the sky,
Beyond spilt stars, and you with Him, were Home.

1941

"Per Ardua Ad Astra"
R.A.F motto By hard work to the stars

A PICTURE

The cool hush of breeze,
In the gray dusk of the north,
And the green half-dusk of the west
Where corn fields glow.
The glimmering fantasies
Of poppies flaunting forth,
Then drooping into rest
I loved to know.
The harvest glimmering
As ripples half asleep
    -    So I atune my love
To softened words:
For here is the dreaming wisdom of
The unchanging things...
And more:- Walk softly lest ye wake
A thousand sleeping things

1941

DAWN SHIPS

I saw a ship of stars
Swing out in the sea of night.
Could'st be the planet Mars
With ripples of spray – star white
As prows cut deep the blue?

Or ghost of a winged ship
Of strange but lovely hue?

The sails are filled and spread
On tides of skies blown high.
    -   The world is full of gray
    -   Away, and the wind blows by
          A wake of slow stars heralds day

1939

WRITTEN AT TRING RESEVOIR

Above my wind swept hair – the gray of evening skies
And 'neath a wet and shining sheet of glimmering steel
Relieved by ruffled waves – from which the swans do rise
Silently and gracefully. Their glistening white must feel
The mist as far into the gathering dusk they sail.
From winds my face is starred with falling drops of rain.
I see this summers's eve a rising fitful gale
Trembling to sweep across the rocks, so boldly lain,
But suddenly as watch dogs called, the thunder lifts.
Now day and silver rain have gone and so the moon
Doth light her lantern in the sky. As slowly drifts
Across her silent face, Gods veil of shining sheen.

1939

COMPARISON

When you were there,

The waters danced laughingly,

The wind blew caressingly

   -   And you held my hand

But on the next day,

The waters heaved sullenly,

The sea gulls wheeled solitarily

   -   And I was alone

1942.

ALL MY TIDES SET SEAWARDS

Across the shining, shallow pooled shore
Gulls wheel, wind driven, like scattered leaves. Adrift
Along swan breasted waves of green do pour
Crashing foam petals, on the beach, high cliffed.

And we run swift, impetous with the wind,
Across the silver sand – down to the sea;
Our ears by mighty thundering are dimmed,
Our eyes are filled by tossing salt-sea's glee.

We gaze and gaze, as in a wond'rous dream,
Upon long waves that lift and swing and roll.
The ceaseless moving seas, unending seem,
To stretch across stark wastes, from pole to pole.

We swim and feel the mighty waters heaving,
They cradle us by motion of their tide,
Whilst round us softly murmers, oceans singing,
A song more sweet than human lips e'er cried.

What wonder that we having heard that crying
Do sometimes dull and empty find the land?
What wonder that we dream till days of dying,
Of tossing, heaving, surges – tide-ribbed sands?

The Isle of Barra

DAWN

Beauty comes,
Sweetly from that naked tree.
While other people sleep
Then dreamy half asleep
I find all beauty In the dawn.
Gull sweeping after gull
Birds' song – clear high flute
Voices – falling mute.
At dawn I heard
A waking bird
Out of the darkness singing.
Beauty comes
Strangely – and I worship.
And gently magic fingers sweep
Across my ears and murmers creep
Softly from that naked tree.
Then all these airs
Rich with change
The wind in the trees
All over the earth is pouring
Solemn music, sinking soaring,
Low to high
Across the sky
I knelt before Beauty
And I saw God smile.
Beauty comes strangely
       God is nigh!

OUR LAND

This is our land: the trees undarkened green
Gleam in far woods: and in the vales between
The gray farms glimmer, clustered in the shade.
Whilst all around the busy fields are bathed
In sunlight, and I hear men's voices near,
As they curse, and smile, and sweat and think of beer,
And drench parched throats with tea. I see

Their clear eyes, strong brown arms, glistening, free.
The cart horse sweating like the man who drives
Plunges for a while out of the sun, and dives
Into the shade, and what cool madness finds!
As the ceaseless clattering mower sweeps the lines,
Then all the hay breaks into laughing eyes
As hidden clover like bright stars arise
The strong sweet smell of hay that fills the wood:
This makes me feel the stubborn hardihood
That's bred in us –freedom – our noblest pride
Which in the heart of Britain never died.

I see the brown line of the straight furrow,
And soft green turf.
A child skipping, a blood horse frolicking on a cold day.
The wind kisses my arms and capering
Sweeps through my hair.

I see your dear eyes smiling, looking gay,
And I bow to
A closing flower or trees at close of day.

Swooping high
And drifting far above the restless clouds,
Like surf crashing
Its ageless tune against a peaceful sky,
I see the birds

IMMORTALITY

These fields, which now lie smiling in the sun,
Were tamed and schooled to harvest long ago
By men whose nameless lives we cannot know,
Who went in silence when their work was done.

Their furrows slowly traced, their crops hard won
Have vanished like some ancient winter's snow,
Their hearts, dispersed in dust, have ceased to glow
Mere random bones declare their race is run.

And yet within the fields there lie in wait
Strange virtues which to them, not us belong.
And as we plod behind the plough, which bares
The gracious earth they wooed, we know the strong
Compulsion laid by them on all their heirs,
And cannot choose but drive our furrows straight.

Anon

17

MATINS

The air is swept with palest gold
Yet, while we watch, it grows
Brighter, finer and more pure.
That sweet-voiced Herald, the dawn wind,
Calls up the sky.
As, with a silver stream of sound
The bells peal clear across the cloisters
And monks, soberly black-gowned,
Move reverently to worship.
The bells have ceased, and soon
The deep-toned chant, melodious and rich,
Blends with the dull, far-away crash of breakers,
On the steps of Day.

1939

ON FALLING ASLEEP IN THE OPEN

Like wave-foam breaking boundless stretch of space,
The lasting clouds pile up with moving grace,
Across the stretching endless depths of sky.
Like silver blooms that live and never die
The magic of a dust of stars are blown.
Like eyes of some dark lovely queen unknown
The winds of space wander thro' the world.
By branches patterns 'gainst the moon unfurled.

Then someone goes between the darkened trees,
As in a mist her feet swirl up the leaves,
And with her comes – flowers in her wind blown hair
Sweet dreams, kind gift of God for mankind's care.

1940

SEA GULLS

Here beside the lonely sea and sky,
Drifting with exultant cries of glee,
Spirits of old sailors drifting by
Haunting their loved home – the living sea –
Wheeling, flashing, swooping by
Silver 'gainst the gray, gray sky
        -Sea gulls!-

The green sea thunders, lifts to crests of snow
The wild sea horses, stamping ceaselessly

And white against the greenness down below
Fly children of the spray, so wild and free!
In the lonely sweeps of sky,
Vagabonds fly crying by
        -Seagulls-!

1941

MEMORIES

Do you still remember
How the breakers swept the shore?
How they used to thunder,
How we loved to hear them roar?

Can you still remember
How the wind whipped up the foam?
How we roamed together
Out where others seldom roam?

Do you still remember
Horses eating from our hand?
How we raced each other
Over heather, over sand?

Do you still remember
Clouds, and how the stars would shine?
Climbing trees with one another
Laughing through the lonely pines?

Do you still remember
Going back to home at night?
How the wolfhound leapt to
Meet us. How the fire was bright?

HORSES

I like their sympathetic faces, and
The nuzzling velvet nose,
That looks for sugar hidden in the hand.

I like the great Clydesdale,
And I like to drive the plough and see them plod
Steadily in front;
Or to clean the feather of their feet, iron shod
With massive heavy shoes.

I like to see a great team standing still,
Muscles gleaming, steam
Rising on the summit of a hill.

To frisk in pure freedom
And caper like a mad thing, the blood horse,
Engine of beauty, like a ripple of swift wind amongst the
grass,
Thing of delight! The cob I like to shine,
Then spanking smartly drive
Clip clop through town and country lane

Sometimes I like to ride
Madly along the sea washed sand and laugh
In happiness to see
The sweep of heaven - white cloud and white surf.

What country is so sweet
As that seen through our horses ears? Again

My mind can see the hunt
-Sheer through the mist into the sun, her mane

A streak of silver light,
As heading not the volley of blind rain
We led the field;
And how like icy wine the eager air
Seemed almost as keen as she,
Who bird-like soared the fences black and bare.
-    They bring old memories   -

I like the arched neck and nostrils fire,
And restless pawing hooves;
Victims of the war-gods fierce embrace
The long line of grey chargers
Tossing their forelocks, edging each for place
Breaking their valiant hearts.
But most of all I like their dreaming eyes
When in the box at night,
I stroke the long and sympathetic face.

1942

A RIDE

Smiling, I galloped up the windy hill,
Sang in the breeze, and loved the beauty there,
And laughed in happiness for all that air
Of clean, sweet, rain drenched earth I drank my fill.

My voice re-echoed madly – low and high –
Then suddenly was quiet again and I
Heard nothing but the thudding of his feet.

My restless blood seemed even then a whim,
I loved it all. Oh God! I loved it all,
Yet even as I joyed I thought might fall,
And even all this loveliness grow dim.
And that was how my soul did light and burn
With shattering ecstasy of those who learn
What 'tis to love – poor fools – what 'tis to love!

1940

COLLEEN

A voice whispers, but no one answers when I call.

A shadow stirs but nothing muzzles to my hand.

I'd bought a lump of sugar – thinking you were there,

Of course I had forgotten.

Your box lies bare, at one side an ugly moke

Eats your hay. I hesitate, and feel alone

In the dark yard, and dry the tears that fall like rain

And still the cold increasing.

The night wind blows, it rustles the trees and makes a noise

Like the sea. Oh that those waves could bring me you!

On the green turf we have flown into the dawn,

Swift as a wave rippling;

And raced the morning wind from cloud to tumbling cloud.

Oft I have whistled, or called you softly here, And seen you

prancing up to me with forelock tossed across your dark

eyes flashing.

With you I learned to love th'exhilerating glow

Of riding on some star bright road at night

Which gleamed stiller than the snow on mountain tops.

We've heard the stars singing,

Shining whiter than the moon between the clouds.

We've shared so many secrets too, some silly things,

Perhaps a tiny foal, that would be born in spring.

But you have gone away.

And all these happy dreams have swiftly passed,

And rolled into a corner of heaven's last

Great sweep of sky. I did not see your feet turn up,

You were not stumbling off

Long in the tooth, blind in the eye, with moulting coat.

-    Your eyes were bright with life,

You danced away, knowing not of death,

You did not live in vain, because my beautiful

It was with you I learned to love all lovely things.

1942

TO YOUTH

I saw you then,

With arms outstretched and face ablaze and gay,

Yearning to be but understood and loved.

And with you once again as on that day

Ran and leapt with you, like some mad thing.

I joyed with you;

To see the thrilling beauty of a horse,

Or feel the pulsing power of his great limbs.

Or lay and heard the wild bees in the gorse

And learned what true companionship can mean,

And then you spoke;

Brave words you said indeed –

And so you went

Right forward, rather finely in this bloody war.

You scarcely seemed to hear the sights that spent

Their cruel anguished cries around your head.

And then you laughed

Aloud, and finding time to play the fool,

Although your friends, with suffering, died around

Somehow you seemed to turn your mind from cruel

Warfare, and laughed, and danced and drank and kissed.

And often swore

When sometimes one would offer sympathy –

And when you stood alone in the cool fields

And tried to find the words you longed to say, they only

thought you sulked and so they left

You all alone.

And that is why they felt such deep surprise

When happ'ning suddenly to come on you

They found you,

Hatred blazing from your eyes

-     Crying as if your soul and heart were dead

Sobbing- those tears that you had never shed.

THIS GREEN LAND

This little land in surf tossed seas - how well
We love the very earth, words cannot tell
How close to all our hearts this country now.
Lord give us strength that we are unafraid,
Though wounded, threatened, make us undismayed.
This ancient country proudly lifts its brow,
This green land must not perish! All in vain
May foes pour out their hell of bombs and fire.
Brave hearts must fight that hell, and never tire;
Brave hearts look up! And look to Him again.
Though torn our fields and battered is the hill,
We'll heal these scars and victor over ill,
With glorious memories on every side
He'll help us build it up as ne'er before
   - Even in the bravest days of happiest yore>
This nations pulsing land – her strong heart's pride.

- O give us love that we may love it much,
- O give us love that we may love thee more!
- 1942

Neva with Land Girl Friend

SPRING – 1940

I sat and watched the world pass by
In never ending stream
And all the people passing nigh
Were so enwrapped in care
That never one amid the crowd
Could'st see the beauty there
Or see the trees against the sky
Or clouds splashed in the blue
Nor could they see the sun on high
And know the world was green
Or see that Spring was on the land
Life springing forth was seen
-     Greeness fading into blue
                    And blue to nothingness.

Yet not so far away they knew
Was being desecrate
A land of free – and red the dew
Was stained, with blood of men
The Spring which once our Lord did choose
For life to flow again
Saw now a river flowing wide
Of death and not of life.
And so the crowd swept by the tide
Was gazing into hell

They did not see the fields about
 Which dear ones loved so well
Their greenness fading into blue
                    And blue to nothingness.

Words That I Love

"Earth's crammed with Heaven &
  Every common bush aflame with God
  But only those who see take off their shoes,
  The rest sit round & pluck blackberries."

PEACE

There is a calm peace in the sea tonight

-   White surf and a gray, gray wave —

There is quiet peace midst the stars above

-   Death white as a silent grave —

And there is peace in my heart within

-   Joy mingled with my breath -

God showed me happiness tonight,

-   He showed me Life past Death.

1940

STRANGE LONELINESS

Sometime, the lilting of a song, once known
In dim forgotten days will stab the heart
A tenderness one hopes to have outgrown
Comes surging back and makes quick tears start.

All in a throng perhaps a voice is heard
Like one we knew – then fades and dies away
And memories that slumbered long are stirred
The mind goes backward to a distant day.

It is if a cloud had veiled the sight.
Which has power to both sadden and to bless,
That brings us sorrow blended with delight
-    And with it strange and haunting loneliness!

1944.

TE DEUM

For Bendix's (automatic washing machine) and piping

water from the tap,

For clean scrubbed floor and lavatories that pull!

For the warmth in an eye or the touch of a hand,

For country loaves that scent the room, and jugs

Of creamy milk and farm house fare – For Hugs

From bairns with rosy cheeks and glowing faces

When, satchels off, come bursting in from school.

For love and sheer delight that bubbles forth

 From baby eyes that smile to greet their brothers.

For the welcome of the kitchen and the clowning of our

bird.

For the gray and faithful nearness of the hound.

For calves with velvet coats and shining noses

That run in health across the frosty ground.

For high spirits and fondness and laughter,

The intangible "something" that goes to make Home.

For the joy when a longed-for letter is in the post

For returning hungry from Church to Sunday roast!

For the sturdy gentleness of hill ponies,

For the light on the loch and the gray stone

Of strong walls that make our Highland Home,

We thank Thee Lord!

1961

Borlum Farm

SNOWDROPS

"Bonny flowers! Bonny flowers - see the flowers like snow!
Hurry up, Mummy come! Quickly 'fore they go!"

Sure enough clumps of them, clean and pure and white
Little face pointing down — smiling eyes alight.

Then one day suddenly, dancing lovely flowers
Calling her, loving her, laughing in the showers!

Later in the kitchen (it is dark outside}
The middle of the table and all the children, pride

Shining, glistening snowdrops, with tippeties of green
Clustered in an egg cup, yet fit for any queen

Or for the king of Heaven, whose gift to us they've been.

MARNIES CROFT

You asked me for a cup of tea

Your croft high in the hills,

But as we sat and drank our fill

Of all that beauty there

We didn't think at all of tea

(It lay neglected cold)

For words can't speak

Nor tongue express

The beauty of such loveliness

Memories

1.   I think my earliest memory is of hiding in the long grass from my brother and sister. I would wait as they searched around, terrified that they would find my hiding place, and then as their voices faded, I became terrified that they may have become bored of looking for me and leave me alone!

2.   One day when I was quite small my father took my sister and myself to lunch, and on the way home he asked us to guess what treat our mother might have in store for us. We were already excited because the lunch had been a treat in itself.

"A horse!" Peggy guessed.
"An elephant!" I guessed.

But we were both disappointed to hear that it was "only a baby!". Which turned out to be my youngest brother David.

3.   I have a memory from early childhood of my Father waking me up and carrying me outside to show me the stars. This memory still gives me feelings of awe wonder and love.

4.   During my early days my brother Peter and sister Peggy felt that I was escaping punishment far too often when we were all caught doing something wrong, because I was the 'little' one. This began to upset them more and more as time went on until they decided to take some action, so they dug a hole in the garden, grabbed hold of me, wishing to plant me in some soil to make me grow! That way they hoped I would receive the punishment I had avoided in the past because of my smaller size, and maybe I would grow a bit more so that I would receive my just rewards in the future!
Picture page 46 to 47.

5.   We were often together as a family and went on Sunday walks would often finish up by climbing a hill somewhere and I remember my father swinging our arms upwards and beaming at us all saying 'isn't God good!'

6.   Because my parents were in the services we were always on the move. On arriving at yet another new school we met the teacher who said to us "Of course you don't have a home yet ", to which my sister replied indignantly " Of course we have – it's just we haven't got a house to put it in yet!"

7.   We were blessed to grow up in an atmosphere of love in which my mother was the heart of the family.

8.   I remember that if we children ever had a disagreement with my father or he was trying to get round us in some way and all else had failed, his trump card was finally to say "Well, after all, I did give you a wonderful mother!" to which we had no answer.

9.   My Father was stationed for some years with the RAF in India, and during the time that our mother visited him there, we children were looked after by our grandparents. I remember an instance where I must have done something wrong and had been denying it for some time, I had finally broken down in tears in front of the large figure of my grandfather, who scooped me up in his strong arms and cradled me on his knee, saying in his deep voice "You may have been a bad wee girl, but you are God's wee girl and HE loves you!"

At that moment I felt so loved and encircled by these everlasting arms around me, and I have always been conscious of it ever since.

Picture page 45 "Everlasting Arms"

10.   In many ways my children taught me not to be frightened of death. The last words spoken to me, by my first born son Jeremy as he died from cancer were, "Mum, I feel so safe, so sure and so loved," and this has stayed with me.

11. I remember my daughter Jennie, also suffering from cancer, aged five, saying "Do you know Mummy, that angels carry children straight to Jesus when they die?" and then after a short silence, saying with some smugness and a huge smile, " Michael is coming for me!" *Picture page 48 "Jennie"*

A last memory

Sandy and I became tenants of a farm and employed German prisoners of war. When the war ended and Winston Churchill was not re-elected as Prime Minister, they were amazed.

'This good man – you write and tell him Germans say so.'

So I did write and the great man sent back a handwritten personal letter saying how touched he was. The letter was stolen but I remember it.

Memory 9 "Everlasting Arms"

Memory 4 "Ordeal"

Memory 4 "All Better"

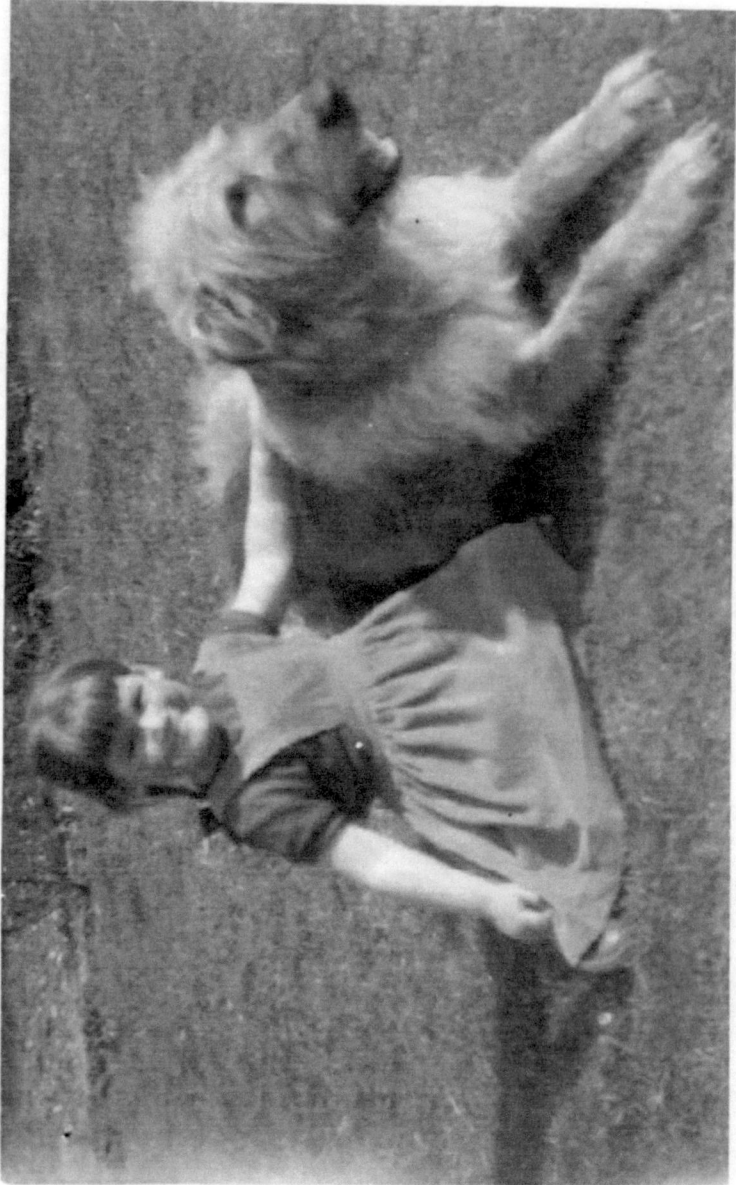

Memory 11 "Jennie"

DISABLED RIDING

Such a lot of my life has been spent with disabled children and adults and their families over the years, and I have so many precious memories of these times. It has been a privilege to share the joy and freedom that riding gave them, and to share the inestimable jewel of friendship with them. Often riding would give them such feelings of freedom it was a pleasure to be there to hear them express themselves. I remember being tapped on the head by one rider who usually used a wheel chair, who said to me, "It's great looking down instead of up!", and hearing a girl with learning difficulties say,   "When I ride, I feel like a normal person."

Another young man, who suffered from autism, and seldom showed emotion, or communicated with people except with his father, was asked to explain what his weekly riding meant to him, because it was thought that he was not benefitting from the sessions. His Father agreed to ask him and returned next week with the answer.
"I love riding a horse, because it makes me feel like dancing!"

It gives me great pleasure when I remember things like this, and the expression on their faces when they say these things. I remember once checking on a small boy; riding a rather large horse, and asking him "Do you feel a bit frightened being so high up?", and he smiled and said emphatically, "No Miss! I feel like a KING!"

However, just because I appeared to be in charge of the group, I was never allowed to feel that I knew it all, being constantly reminded by a friend with Downs syndrome "Och Grannie Haig, you're just no wise!"
Another time at a Gymkana he ran up to me waving his rosette saying, "Look Grannie! I've got a rosette with the biggest name on it, and its …… P A R T I C I P A T I O N ! "

Another friend, Trevor, who was one of our regular riders at Borlum during this time, had a favourite horse, Eilean Lass, who was much loved by him over the years, and when the time came that she died, Trevor was absolutely devastated. On that day, when his bus arrived to take his group home, Trevor was not to be found anywhere, and people searched high and low for him around the stables. Eventually Trevor was found climbing the hill behind Borlum with a carrot in his hand, on his way to offer the carrot to Eilan Lass, "In Heaven!"

"Joy" William (unable to see or hear) meets Abigall

Emily, Becki and Tom Thumb H.E.A.R.T

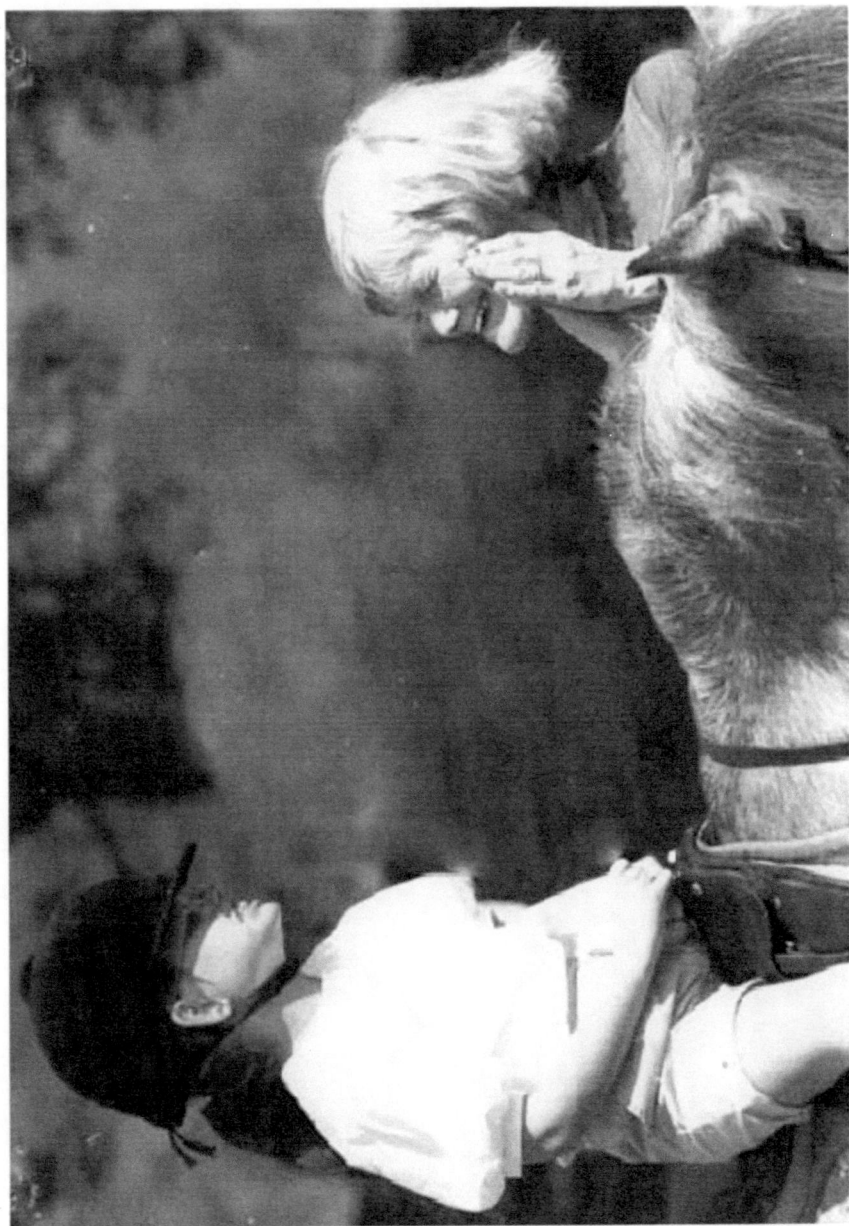

First ride

"Beannachd Leibh"

Gaelic for "Blessings with you!"

from a land girl who's grown older.

(H.E.A.R.T)
Highland Equine And Riding Therapy

A charity registered in Scotland number SC043483 this little book of poems is being sold in aid of H.E.A.R.T. We currently provide financial support to forty riders, children and adults with disabilities or long-term illness to enable then to enjoy the many proven benefits of riding and interacting with horses and ponies.

We aim to help those with physical disabilities such as cerebral palsy; mental illnesses; learning disabilities; autistic spectrum disorders and other conditions such as Post Traumatic Stress Disorder.

The organisation will use the excellent facilities at Highland Riding Centre, which for almost 40 years has provided these activities and which has a wealth of relevant experience – amongst both is two-legged and four-legged staff! Chief Instructor is Pauline Corker, a fellow of the RDA, who holds BHSII and RDASI qualifications and who is highly respected in the field of riding for those with disabilities. H.E.A.R.T is however totally independent of the riding centre.

Anyone interested in helping in any capacity or seeking support should in the first instance contact Margaret Crichton on 01456 45069